261498

Why can't I...
slide down a rainbow?

and other questions
about light

Sally Hewitt

Thameside Press

Distributed in the United States by
Smart Apple Media
1980 Lookout Drive
North Mankato, MN 56003

Text by Sally Hewitt 2002

ISBN 1-930643-70-5

Library of Congress Control Number 2002 141317

Series editor: Jean Coppendale
Designers: Jacqueline Palmer and Fanny Level
Picture researcher: Terry Forshaw
Consultant: Helen Walters

Printed in Hong Kong

10 9 8 7 6 5 4 3 2 1

Picture acknowledgments:
(T) = Top, (B) = Bottom, (L) = Left, (R) = Right, (B/G) = Background,
(C) = Center

Front Cover & 16-17 (B/G) © Darrell Gulin/Corbis; 3 (T) & 26-27 (T) Chrysalis
Images; 4 (TR), 19 (TL) & (CR) © Digital Vision; 5 (B) & 26-27 (B) Chrysalis
Images; 7 (B/G) © Peter Johnson/Corbis; 9 © Robin Scagell/Galaxy Picture
Library; 10 (B/G) © Digital Vision; 11 inset (B/G) © Robin Scagell/Galaxy Picture
Library; 13 (B/G) © Richard Hamilton/Corbis; 14 inset © Japack
Company/Corbis 15 (B/G) © Japack Company/Corbis; 19 (BR) © Digital Vision;
21 (R) © Brendan Byrne/Digital Vision; 25 © Ian West/Bubbles.

All other photography Ray Moller.

Contents

When you open your eyes, you can see what is going on all around you.

What can you see now?
You can see the words and pictures in this book.

What else can you see? Can you see **colors**, shapes, and things moving?

You can see all these things because of **light**. Sunlight shines on Earth and lights it up.

4

We can't see in the dark **night** when our part of Earth isn't facing the Sun. So, we turn on electric lights or light candles to light up the dark.

But what is light?

This book will show you that light is a mixture of all the colors of the rainbow. It will also tell you how shadows are made and why you will never run as fast as light.

Why can't I see with my eyes shut?

Because your eyes must be open to let in light.

You need light to see.

Light shines into your eyes through the black holes called **pupils**.

Why is it dark at night?

Because we can't see the **Sun** at night.

The Earth spins around and around in space.

When the part of the Earth where you are turns to face the sun, it is **day**.

When it turns to face away from the Sun, it is night.

Why does the Moon seem to change shape?

Because the Moon is lit up by the Sun.

The Moon is a big ball of rock with no light of its own.

The Moon always stays the same shape but as it moves around the Earth, we can only see the part that is lit up by the Sun.

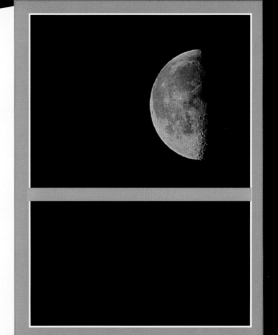

Why can't I see stars in the day?

Because sunlight is much brighter than starlight.

The Sun is the nearest star to Earth.

All the other **stars** are so far away that we can only see them at night as dots of twinkling light.

Why can't I catch a star?

Because stars are too big and hot, and too far away.

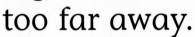

Stars are gigantic balls of burning gas.

They are so far away that light from the stars can take millions of years to travel through space to Earth.

Why can't I run away from my own shadow?

Because when you move, your **shadow** moves with you.

You make your own shadow because the Sun cannot shine through you.

On a sunny day, you make a dark patch nearly the same shape as yourself where the sun can't shine.

Why can't I see my shadow on a cloudy day?

Because the Sun can't shine brightly through clouds.

Clouds only let through a little sunlight.

Sunlight on a cloudy day is too dull to make a shadow. 13

Why does a light bulb glow?

Because the wire inside it gets very hot.

When you turn on a light switch, electricity passes through the wire.

The wire glows when it heats up and gives out light.

Why does the sea sparkle?

Because light bounces off the sea like a ball off a wall.

When **rays** of sunlight hit the sea, they bounce off the ripples and waves in lots of different directions. We then see sparkles of light.

15

Why can't I slide down a rainbow?

Because a **rainbow** is an arch of light.

You see a rainbow when sunlight shines through raindrops and splits into seven different colors.

The colors are red, orange, yellow, green, blue, indigo, and violet.

If you tried to slide down a rainbow, you would fall right through it.

Why can't the whole world be my favorite color?

Because light is all the colors of the rainbow.

Everything has its own color because of the way light bounces off it.

Different things bounce different colors into your eyes.

A leaf looks green because it bounces green light into your eyes. It takes in all the other colors and you don't see them.

18

Why can't I see colors in the dark?

Because we only see colors when enough light bounces into our eyes.

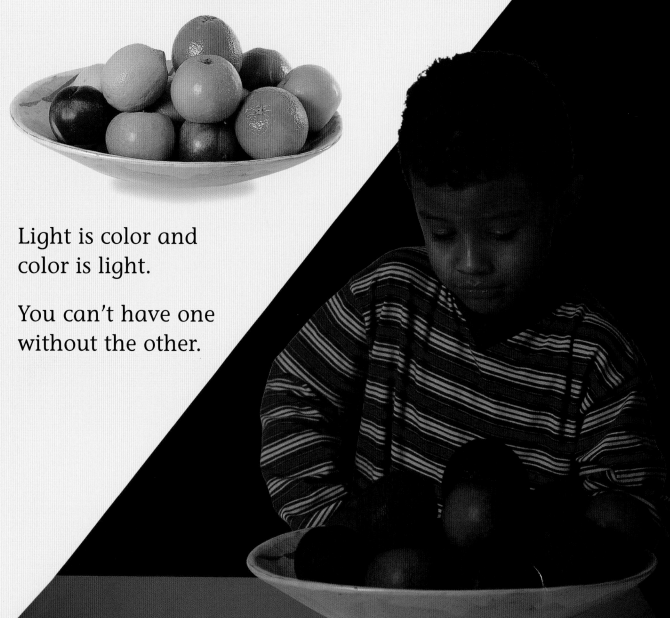

Light is color and color is light.

You can't have one without the other.

Why doesn't my jacket glow in the dark?

Because your jacket isn't made of the right material.

Some material glows in the light of car headlights, making the person wearing it easy to see.

Why do I look funny in a fairground mirror?

Because fairground **mirrors** aren't flat.

They bulge in and out and make some parts of you look stretched while other parts of you look very squashed.

Why is my reflection reversed in a mirror?

Because a mirror bounces your **reflection** straight back at you.

When you wave your right hand at a mirror, it looks like you are waving your left hand.

Why can't my flashlight shine around corners?

Because light travels in straight lines called rays.

Rays of light are straight.

They can't go around corners and they can't shine through solid things.

Why do my arms look bendy under water?

Because light bends as it goes through water.

Light travels more slowly through water than it does through air.

This makes your arms look bent.

Why can't I move as fast as light?

Because light is the fastest mover in the universe.

4

Nothing moves faster than light. Light travels at 186,000 miles a second.

However hard you trained, you could never run as fast as that!

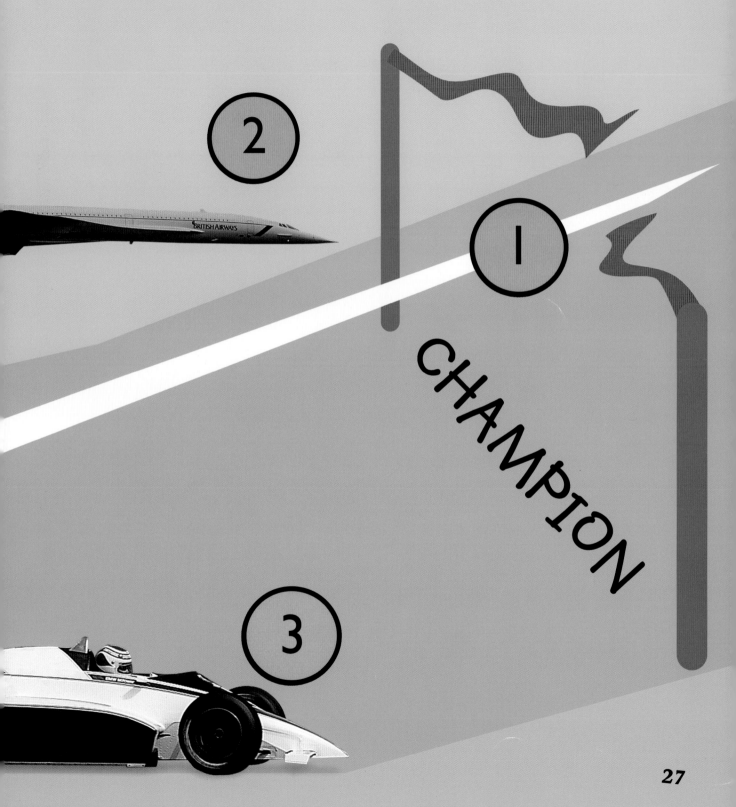

CHAMPION

Light words

colors There are seven colors in light: red, orange, yellow, green, blue, indigo, and violet. We see colors when the things around us bounce one or more of the colors of light back into our eyes.

day When the Sun shines on your part of Earth and lights it up, it is day.

indigo A deep violet-blue.

light Light is the opposite of dark. The Sun gives the Earth its light and lets us see the things around us.

mirrors Mirrors are flat pieces of glass with silver backing. You see yourself in the mirror when light bounces off its shiny surface.

night When your part of Earth is facing away from the Sun, it becomes dark and we say it is nighttime.

pupils Your pupils are the black circles in your eyes. They are holes that let light into your eyes so you can see.

rainbow A rainbow is an arch of light in the sky. When sunlight shines through raindrops, the water bends the light and splits it into seven colors. We see a rainbow.

rays Light travels in straight lines called rays. Rays of light cannot shine through solid things or go around corners.

reflection Your reflection is the picture you see of yourself in a mirror or any other shiny surface. Your reflection seems to be reversed.

shadow A shadow is the dark patch that is made when rays of light hit something solid and cannot pass through it.

stars Stars are gigantic balls of burning gas in space.

Sun The Sun is our nearest star. It gives the Earth heat and light.

Activities

Some of these things glow with light and some don't. Can you find all the things that glow?

- light bulb
- diamond
- candle
- fan
- fire
- window
- Sun

- stone
- stars
- mirror
- flashlight
- spoon
- cloud
- pencil

- lightning
- book
- match
- glowworm
- desk lamp
- water

These are six of the colors in a rainbow...

red, orange, yellow, green, blue, and violet

Match each of these fruits to a color of the rainbow...

blueberry, banana, tangerine, plum, lime, and strawberry

Notes for parents and teachers

Children know they can't slide down a rainbow, but they may not know the reason why. Spend some time together thinking about the questions in this book and the possibilities they raise before reading the simple, factual answers. You may like to try out the following activities with your child. They will reinforce what you have learned about light and give you plenty to discuss.

Mixing colors

You can make all the colors of the rainbow by mixing the primary colors (red, yellow, and blue).

Assemble bright red, yellow, and blue paints, a paint brush, a container of clean water, an old plate for mixing the paints, and some white paper.

Mix red and yellow to make orange, yellow and blue to make green, and red and blue to make violet.

Use all the colors to paint a rainbow.

Now find out what happens when you mix all the colors together.

Shadow puppets

Turn off all the lights and draw the curtains to make a room as dark as you can. Shine a powerful flashlight onto a wall. Show your child how to make different shapes with their hands to cast the shadows of a butterfly, a rabbit, and a dog onto the wall.

Sparkling mobile

Collect all sorts of shiny things such as silver foil, colored glass beads, tinsel, and Christmas baubles. Dangle them from a clothes hanger and hang it somewhere where it will catch the light and move in the breeze. Watch the mobile sparkle and throw reflections onto the walls around it.

Index